Is a GOD a Committee?

Is GOD a Committee?

What the Bible Teaches About the Godhead

By Gerald Wheeler

Southern Publishing Association, Nashville, Tennessee

Dedicated to
MOM

Edited by Richard Coffen
Designed by Dean Tucker
Cover photo by John Guider Studio

Printed in U.S.A.

In addition to the King James Version of the Bible and the Revised Standard Version, the following versions have been quoted:

The New Testament in Modern English. Copyright, J. B. Phillips, 1958. Used by permission of The Macmillan Company.

TEV, Today's English Version of the New Testament. Copyright, American Bible Society, 1966, 1971.

Table of **CONTENTS**

1

How Many Is God?

$1+1+1=1$? Can one-third person plus one-third person plus one-third person equal one person? Confusing? Sound like one of those modern math problems involving sets your children might have studied in school? It's not. Instead it represents descriptions by opponents of the frequently misunderstood and violently attacked Christian doctrine of the Godhead—more commonly termed the Trinity.

From the time of Christ, church leaders have disagreed over the nature of God. However, God declares, "My thoughts are not your thoughts, neither are your ways my ways, says the Lord. For as the heavens are higher than the earth, so are my ways higher than your ways and my thoughts than your thoughts" (Isaiah 55:8, 9, RSV*). The Creator is always greater than His created beings. His nature is naturally more complex than man's. Yet, characteristically, the human mind wants to understand the universe and the Being who made it in the first place.

---

* Unless otherwise noted, Biblical passages are quoted from the Revised Standard Version.

Through the centuries many have attempted to explain God, but because man's mind and intellect are far below God's, his descriptions can be only incomplete and often misleading. The early Christian church had to grapple with a growing revelation of God. They had to answer such questions as: What was Jesus Christ's relationship to the Father? Was He equal with God or a lesser being? Had He always existed, or had the Father created Him? And the Holy Spirit—was He another being or just a power and influence the Father and Son used? If the Father, Son, and Holy Spirit were three separate beings, what was their relationship to each other? Or, perhaps, could they actually be one and the same being?

In its attempts to explain the Godhead and its various members, the church tried out a number of erroneous approaches, most of which still persist in one disguise or another. They include:

1. *Adoptionism*. Those who advocated adoptionism believed that by a special divine decree the virgin Mary gave birth to a man named Jesus. After a thorough testing, Jesus received supernatural powers from the Holy Spirit at His baptism. As a reward for His sterling character and exemplary life, God raised Him from the dead and elevated Him into the Godhead. Christ was a man who became God. Several groups, including one fast-growing denomination, still teach forms of adoptionist theories. Some modern theologians see Christ as nothing more than the only man who completely opened Himself to the love of God.

2. *Tritheism*. Tritheists believe in three distinct Gods who do not form one Godhead, but They are separate. The concept borders on polytheism.

3. *Sabellianism or modalism*. Sabellius, a third-century religious thinker, believed that God was essentially one but took different forms for specific purposes. At first He was the Father, then incarnated Himself as the Son, and now has the role of the Holy Spirit. Strangely enough, this misconception has seen a revival in what some people call Christo-unitarianism. Some members of the Jesus People movement, which began during the early 1970's taught that the Father, the Son, and the Holy Spirit were one and the same person and that God's true name was Jesus Christ. Some Pentecostal groups hold a similar belief

4. *Arianism*. The most long-lasting misunderstanding of the Godhead began when Arius, a church leader of Alexandria, argued in AD 313 that Christ was the first created being and thus subordinate to the Father. He propounded that although Christ created all other living things, He had not always existed as had the Father. He was the Father's inferior. The debate Arius started divided Christianity into two warring camps for centuries. From Arianism has developed Unitarianism and a number of Christian sects. Some totally deny that Christ was anything more than an exceptionally good man, the model human being.

Christo-unitarianism among the Jesus movement and the continued existence of Unitarianism and other Arian groups illustrate that many people still have a hard time accepting or understanding the Godhead. The misconceptions outlined in this chapter keep reappearing in the church. Are the critics of the doctrine of the Godhead right when they claim that the doctrine of the Trinity is a pagan heresy derived from some three-headed Babylonian god? What can the Christian actually think about the Trinity? What does the Bible teach about it? And does it really matter what anyone believes about the whole thing?

2

The Bible and the Trinity

The critics are correct when they say that *Trinity* does not appear in the Bible. As far as we know, Theophilus of Antioch first used this term during the second century. He derived it from the Greek word *trias* meaning three. The King James Version of the Bible, however, has translated several cognate Greek words "Godhead." The words include *theion* (Acts 17:29), "divinity," "the Deity"; *theiotēs* (Romans 1:20), "divine nature," "divinity"; and *theotēs* (Colossians 2:9), "deity," "divinity." But because the Bible does not specifically use the word *Trinity* does not mean that it lacks the concept.

The word *millennium* never appears in the Bible, coming instead from the Latin *mille annus,* "a thousand years." But Scripture does teach the concept in Revelation 19 and 20. Many anti-Trinitarians reject the doctrine of the Godhead because the Bible fails to use the term Trinity, yet they hold some version of the millennium—another term that does not appear in Scripture.

Is the Trinity a New Testament or even a post-apostolic invention, especially since the Old Testament proclaims, "Hear, O Israel: The Lord our God is one Lord" (Deuteronomy 6:4)? Obviously the Jews did and still do believe in only one God, not three equal ones or anything else. Yet a careful study of the Old Testament does not rule out the Godhead, but in fact, even hints at it.

Echad, the Hebrew word translated "one" in Deuteronomy 6:4, also appears in Genesis 2:24 where God stated that a man should leave his parents and "cleave" to his wife, becoming "one flesh." Numbers 13:23 employs it in referring to the cluster of grapes the Hebrew spies brought back from the land of Canaan. In both cases the word shows a composite unity: two separate individuals comprising "one flesh" and a multitude of grapes forming "one" or a "single" cluster. The Godhead has three members, but it is one in a unity more close than we can comprehend.

Chapters 18 and 19 of the Book of Genesis offer an interesting clue to the Godhead. They describe how the Lord and two angels walked into the camp of the patriarch Abraham one day. The patriarch fed them, then the angels went on ahead to the city of Sodom to warn Abraham's nephew Lot of the city's impending destruction. Abraham pleaded with God to spare the city if it contained at least ten righteous people. Unfortunately, it did not, and "the *Lord rained upon* Sodom and upon Gomorrah brimstone and fire *from the Lord out of heaven*" (Genesis 19:24). The passage strongly implies at least two individuals—One on earth and One in heaven—called "Lord."

A common word the Hebrew Scriptures used for God was '*Elohim,* which usually occurs in the plural form. Sometimes it has a singular verb, perhaps indicating that the Old Testament writers conceived of the Godhead as a discreet unit. The Genesis Creation account contains '*Elohim,* and at one point God says, " 'Let *us* make man in *our* image, after *our* likeness' " (Genesis 1:26). After man's spiritual fall, God commented, " 'Behold, the man has become like one of us, knowing good and evil' " (Genesis 3:22). Some argue that the use of the plural '*Elohim* merely indicates God's majesty, much as kings once employed the imperial "we." Yet Scripture clearly indicates that more than one Divine Being was present at the creation of the earth. John 1:2, 3 states that the Word—Christ—"was in the beginning with God; all things were made through him, and without him was not anything made that was made." Colossians 1:16 also emphasizes Christ's role in creation. Genesis 1:2 gives evidence for the additional presence of the Holy Spirit.

In the vision of his anointing as a prophet, Isaiah "heard the voice of the Lord saying, 'Whom shall I send, and who will go for *us?*' " (Isaiah 6:8). Elsewhere in the Book of Isaiah we find the passage, " 'Draw near to me, hear this: from the beginning I have not spoken in secret, from the time it came to be I have been there ["there am I," KJV].' And now the Lord God has sent me and his Spirit" (Isaiah 48:16). The RSV puts quotation marks after *there,* making it appear Isaiah said the last part of the passage instead of God, but since the original Hebrew text had no quotation marks, it is an interpretive decision. The context of the chapter indicates that the "me" does not have to be the prophet speaking, but it could just as well be the Lord. If that is the case, we have two Lords and the Spirit mentioned together. At the least it is one of dozens of passages in the Old Testament that mention the Spirit of the Lord.

In the New Testament, Christ quoted a passage from the Old Testament, Psalm 110:1. Christ "said to them, 'How is it then that David, inspired by the Spirit, calls him [the son of David, that is, Christ, according to verse 42] Lord, saying, "The Lord said to my Lord, Sit at my right hand, till I put thy enemies under thy feet"?' " (Matthew 22:43, 44). In verse 44 the words translated *Lord* both come from *Kurios,* the Greek equivalent of *Yahweh,* the most sacred of the Hebrew names for God. (The root form of Yahweh—the four consonants known as the Tetragrammaton—is commonly transliterated "Jehovah.") The literal Greek of Matthew's passage reads: "[The] Lord said to my Lord." The manuscripts of the New Testament books use *Kurios* both to translate the Hebrew word *Yahweh* and to refer to Christ. For another example, compare Psalm 102:22, 25-28 with Hebrews 1:10-12. (We could, if space permitted, cite many more.) The early Christians suffered persecution and death rather than call the Roman emperors *Kurios.* To them it meant referring to Caesar as *Yahweh,* the Lord God Almighty.

Being a compilation of writings by different authors, the Bible rarely deals systematically with any topic. Thus, the New Testament, like the Old, only alludes to the Trinity. As with most doctrines, the Bible student must put all the Scriptural passages together to see what the Bible teaches about the Godhead.

Many have advocated 1 John 5:7 (King James Version) as a direct statement of the Trinity, but a study of Biblical manuscripts indicates that the text apparently dates from the fifteenth century. It does not show up in more ancient Bible manuscripts.

Christ, however, mentioned the threefold Godhead when He instructed His followers to " 'go therefore and make disciples of all nations, baptizing them in the *name* of the Father and of the Son and of the Holy Spirit' " (Matthew 28:19). Notice that "name" is singular, indicating that Christ conceived of them as one unit.

The following passages also mention the three members of the Godhead:

"And when Jesus was baptized, he went up immediately from the water, and behold, the heavens were opened and he saw the Spirit of God descending like a dove, and alighting on him; and lo, a voice from heaven, saying, 'This is my beloved Son, with whom I am well pleased' " (Matthew 3:16, 17).

" 'And I [Christ] will pray the Father, and he will give you another Counselor, to be with you for ever, even the Spirit of truth, whom the world cannot receive, because it neither sees him nor knows him; you know him, for he dwells with you, and will be in you' " (John 14:16, 17).

" 'But the Counselor, the Holy Spirit, whom the Father will send in my [Christ's] name, he will teach you all things, and bring to your remembrance all that I have said to you' " (John 14:26).

" 'But when the Counselor comes, whom I shall send to you from the Father, even the Spirit of truth, who proceeds from the Father, he will bear witness to me' " (John 15:26).

"The grace of the Lord Jesus Christ and the love of God and the fellowship of the Holy Spirit be with you all" (2 Corinthians 13:14).

"For through him [Christ] we both have access in one Spirit to the Father" (Ephesians 2:18).

"But you, beloved, build yourselves up on your most holy faith; pray in the Holy Spirit; keep yourselves in the love of God; wait for the mercy of our Lord Jesus Christ unto eternal life" (Jude 20, 21).

Instead of being a new heresy, the doctrine of the Trinity is the most fundamental religious principle, since the Godhead existed before anything else.

The best way to discover the Biblical teaching about the Trinity is to see what Scripture has to say about the subject. The next several chapters will explore what the Bible writers disclose about each member of the Godhead.

3

God the Father

God is love, and always has been (1 John 4:8). But fallen human nature does not usually grasp God's love for mankind. By the time of Christ the Jewish religious leaders had so strongly emphasized God's justice that the people thought of Him almost exclusively as a fussy God concerned with legalistic trivia.

God had not hidden His love for His people. In fact, He constantly demonstrated it and reminded man of it. He told Israel, " 'I have loved you with an everlasting love' " (Jeremiah 31:3). Through the prophet Hosea He declared, "I led them with cords of compassion, with the bands of love" (Hosea 11:4). But the nation of Israel did not seem to understand God's loving overtures. So God the Father sent a living demonstration of His nature—Jesus Christ.

The Fatherhood of God was one of Christ's greatest themes. He constantly stressed it. In the Gospel of John alone we find 114 references to the Father. But Christ did not introduce a new doctrine. God's role as Father appears in the Old Testament also. (See Deuteronomy 1:31; 8:5; 14:1; 2 Samuel

7:14; Psalms 2:7; 89:26; 103:13; Isaiah 1:2; Hosea 11:1; Malachi 1:6; 3:17.) TheLord had told David to cry to Him, " ' "Thou art my Father" ' " (Psalm 89:26). Christ would show the whole world what that Father was like. When the apostle Philip asked Him, " 'Lord, show us the Father,' " Christ replied, " 'He who has seen me has seen the Father' " (John 14:8, 9).

What did Christ reveal about the Father? First, as we have already stated, that He was a God of love. "For God so loved the world that he gave his only Son, that whoever believes in him should not perish but have eternal life" (John 3:16). Christ's whole life exemplified love, and all that He did fulfilled His Father's loving will (John 5:30). Everything Christ did, the Father would have done.

Second, Christ showed that the Father was accessible. In the Lord's Prayer (Matthew 6:9-13) He taught us to approach the Father with our needs and requests because the Father listens for our petitions. Anything we ask of Him that is good for us, He will give to us (John 16:23). God the Father is not some distant being, unconcerned with what happens to humanity. He seeks to be as close to us as does any human father. And our relationship with Him should be as intimate as that of father and child. Christ used His relationship with His Father as the example of the kind of relationship His followers should have with the Father and each other (John 17:11, 23). The human father actively involves himself in his children's life. God the Father wants to be just as immersed in our lives.

God is our Father because He created us. But even more important than that, He is our Father through re-creation—through the process of spiritual rebirth. As Christ said, "Truly, truly, I say to you, unless one is born anew, he cannot see the kingdom of God" (John 3:3). To some who had not been born anew, He stated, "If God were your Father, you would love me" (John 8:42). God was not the Pharisees' Father because they had not experienced spiritual rebirth.

By believing in Christ we become children of God (John 1:12). God adopts us and we receive the Holy Spirit (Romans 8:15-17). Such adoption is possible because Christ redeemed us (Galatians 4:5-7).

The Father, as part of the Godhead, shares with the other members of the Godhead certain basic characteristics which set them apart from all other beings in the universe. They are:

1. *Immortality*. God has no beginning or end.

> Psalm 90:2
> Psalm 102:24-27

2. *Omnipresence*. God is spiritually present everywhere.

> 1 Kings 8:27
> Psalm 139:7-12
> Jeremiah 23:23, 24
> Amos 9:2, 3
> Acts 17:27, 28
> Hebrews 4:13

3. *Omniscience*. God has all knowledge. He sees and knows what goes on everywhere.

> Job 37:16
> Psalm 147:4, 5
> Isaiah 40:28
> Isaiah 46:9, 10
> Daniel 2:20-22
> Romans 11:33
> 1 John 3:20

4. *Omnipotence*. God can accomplish what He wills.

> Jeremiah 32:17
> Daniel 4:35
> Matthew 19:26
> James 4:12-15

5. *Immutability*. God does not change in character or nature.

> 1 Samuel 15:29
> Psalm 33:11
> Malachi 3:6
> Hebrews 1:12
> James 1:17

Besides the five fundamental characteristics listed above, God the Father and the other members of the Godhead have many moral attributes, a number of which we cite on the next page.

Holiness—Psalm 99:9
Righteousness—Ezra 9:15
Mercy—Isaiah 55:7
Faithfulness and truth—Deuteronomy 32:4
Purity—Habakkuk 1:13
Love—1 John 4:8

Comparing how Scripture applies these and other attributes not only to the Father but also to Christ and to the Holy Spirit confirms both the reality of the Godhead and the equality and deity of the Son and the Spirit.

As we stated before, some down through the centuries have claimed that the Father, the Son, and the Holy Spirit are really one Being who assumes different natures for the various tasks He needs to perform. Certain members of the recent Jesus movement have taught that the Father, the Son, and the Holy Spirit were the same Person and His true name was Jesus Christ. Yet the Bible clearly indicates that the Father and Christ are distinct, separate personalities who exist simultaneously.

As Christ rose from the water at His baptism, "he saw the heavens opened and the Spirit descending upon him like a dove; and a voice came from heaven, 'Thou art my beloved Son; with thee I am well pleased' " (Mark 1:10, 11). Notice a voice —the Father—called Christ His Son, and the Holy Spirit symbolized His presence through the form of the dove. All three members of the Godhead were present.

Shortly after Christ's transfiguration on the

mount, "a bright cloud overshadowed them, and a voice from the cloud said, 'This is my beloved Son, with whom I am well pleased; listen to him' " (Matthew 17:5). John 12:28 records a third time the Father spoke during Christ's life on earth. Since Christ was visibly present in each case, for Christ to be also the Father and the Spirit He would have had to perform some kind of trick or illusion, which raises grave ethical and theological questions. Christ in the Garden of Gethsemane and on many other recorded occasions prayed to the Father. Did He pray to Himself? Did He have some kind of divine split personality? The most consistent conclusion from Scripture is that the Father and the Son are separate beings.

4

God the Son

Several lines of evidence indicate that Jesus Christ is just as much Yahweh (Jehovah) God as is the Father. First, as mentioned in the previous chapter, one can compare how Scripture applies the same descriptions and attributes to both the Father and the Son. From the dozens we could offer, we will cite only a few because of limited space.

God the Father

A. Isaiah 10:21
   Jeremiah 32:18
   Both speak of the Lord as "mighty God."

B. Isaiah 43:11
   "I, I am the Lord, and besides me there
   is no savior."

C. Isaiah 44:6
   " 'I am the first and I am the last; besides me
   there is no god.' "

D. Genesis 1:1
   "In the beginning God created."

E. Malachi 3:6
   " 'I the Lord do not change.' "

F. Deuteronomy 32:4
   " 'A God . . . without iniquity.' "

Jesus Christ

A. Isaiah 9:6
   Messianic prophecy speaking of "Mighty God."

B. Titus 1:4
   "Christ Jesus our Savior."

   Acts 4:12
   "Salvation in no one else."

C. Revelation 1:17
   Revelation 22:13
   "First and last"

D. John 1:3
   "All things were made through him."

E. Hebrews 13:8
   "Jesus Christ is the same yesterday and today
   and for ever."

F. Hebrews 4:15
  "Without sinning."

The examples presented represent only a minute fraction of those the reader can find, for the Bible is full of this kind of support for the deity of Christ.

Christ permitted people to worship Him. Yet to Satan He quoted Old Testament scripture which taught that created beings should worship no one except God (Matthew 4:9, 10). To worship another being was blasphemy. The Bible contains several instances of men and even angels refusing homage to themselves. (See Acts 10:25, 26; 14:10-15; Revelation 19:10; 22:8, 9.) Yet Christ accepted from men and women worship that went far beyond such homage as we may conscientiously give another human being or angel. (See Matthew 14:33; 15:25; 28:9; Hebrews 1:6.) If Christ were not fully God, He allowed men to commit blasphemy and idolatry.

The apostle Thomas, after Christ's resurrection, called Him "my Lord and my God" (John 20:28). Christ did *not* correct Thomas for referring to Him as God and Lord. Instead He commented on the apostle's faith. Remember that the word translated "Lord" is *Kurios,* the word that Greek-speaking Jews used for *Yahweh*.

As mentioned before, the early Christians chose death rather than to call the Roman emperor *Kurios*. *Kurios* was more than just a term of respect as we now use "Mister," "sir," or "the honorable one." It was the Greek word used for the most sacred name of God—*Yahweh*—and they applied it to Christ.

Jesus was both Lord and Christ, that is, *Yahweh* and Messiah. He was "Lord of all" (Acts 10:36) and "Lord of lords" (Revelation 17:14). Paul wrote that every being should confess that Christ is *Kurios*. The early Christians called Christ *Kurios* only because the Holy Spirit inspired them to (1 Corinthians 12:3).

God the Father commanded all the angels to worship Christ at His birth into the world. God is jealous of His worship and would not permit any created beings to worship anything except God Himself. The second commandment and the entire Old Testament clearly condemn any kind of idolatry.

The apostle John refers to Christ as the "Word, . . . and without him was not anything made that was made." The Jewish Targums, Aramaic paraphrases and commentaries on the books of the Old Testament, often used *Word* as a circumlocution for the divine name of God. The Targumists were particularly concerned about the sanctity of God's name, and they often substituted "Word," "Glory," and "Presence" for Yahweh. The Neophyti Targum used "the Word of the Lord" in the Genesis account of creation as the One who did the actual creating.

Apparently John used a term that Jewish readers would understand as a pious substitute for references to Yahweh and applied it to Christ. (According to Martin McNamara, the bulk of the Palestinian Targum, of which the Neophyti Targum is a part, comes from pre-Christian times.) To call Christ the Word was to equate Him with Yahweh.

The Bible records several instances where Christ directly, clearly, claimed to be *Yahweh* God. John 8 describes one of Christ's many encounters with the Jewish leaders. They had accused Him of demon possession, which He denied. He said that anyone who kept His teachings would never see death. The Jews pointed out that even their greatest ancestor, Abraham, had died, along with all the prophets. "Are you greater than our father Abraham?" they demanded in verse 53.

Christ replied, "Your father Abraham rejoiced that he was to see my day; he saw it and was glad" (verse 56). The Jews interpreted Christ's answer as a claim to having personally seen Abraham alive. Aghast, they retorted that He was less than fifty years old, meaning that He hadn't even reached the Jewish retirement age (verse 57). Then Jesus said, "Truly, truly, I say to you, before Abraham was, *I am*" (in the Greek, *ego eimi*) (verse 58).

It was a most unusual response. Could the ungrammatical "I am" be a mistake in copying? Hardly, for the earliest manuscripts all have *ego eimi*. If the apostle John mistranslated Christ's Aramaic statement, we cannot trust the Bible, a position which abundant other evidence contradicts. And surely someone would have caught the *ego eimi* during or soon after John's time if it were not right. Obviously, Christ deliberately meant to say "I am." Why? Notice what the Jews immediately did. "So they took up stones to throw at him" (verse 59).

Stoning was the Jewish punishment for blasphemy. How had Christ committed such an act in their eyes? "I am" was definite reference to God Himself as recorded in the Old Testament. The Alexandrian Jewish colony made a Greek translation of the Old Testament (the Septuagint) before Christ's birth. The New Testament generally followed the Septuagint translation when quoting from the Old Testament, and it used *ego eimi* for Yahweh's "I am" of Deuteronomy 32:39 and Isaiah 43:11. Christ claimed to be God Yahweh, and the Jews knew it. He had used an expression in a way that the Jewish mind and religious culture could interpret in no other way.

Hebrew law legalized stoning in only five cases: (1) spiritism (Leviticus 20:27); (2) cursing or blaspheming (Leviticus 24:10-23); (3) false prophets who lead others to worship idols (Deuteronomy 13:1-10); (4) a stubborn son (Deuteronomy 21:18-21); and (5) adultery and rape (Deuteronomy 22:21-24 and Leviticus 20:10).

The only legal grounds the Pharisees could have possibly used as an excuse for stoning Christ was blasphemy, misusing God's sacred name by claiming to be God Himself. Some critics explain their violent reaction because He called them children of the devil (John 8:44). Yet it is unlikely that such legalistic and law-oriented people would behave in such a manner except under the most extreme provocation. Jewish law did not permit stoning for insults. Christ was popular with the masses, and the Hebrew leaders knew the trouble that would result if they stoned Christ without ample and legal cause. In addition, they had not attempted to stone Him in other cases (Matthew 12:34; 23:33) when He called them sons of vipers. Instead, in John 8 the Jewish religious authorities clearly recognized that Christ was claiming godhood for Himself. A similar incident appears in John 10:33 where they again tried to stone Christ *and accused Him of making Himself God*. If the Jews were under a mistaken impression, surely Scripture would have made some indication of this vital point. The Bible writers often clarified other statements which they thought their readers might misunderstand.

Christ also used the expression *ego eimi* in John 13:19 where He told the disciples about the signs of the destruction of Jerusalem and of His second coming. He stated that He was telling them future events so that when they occurred, Christ's followers would know that He was the great "I am" of Exodus 3:14 and Isaiah 44:6. Only Yahweh can really claim the ability to foretell future events with accuracy. (See Isaiah 46:9, 10; 48:5-8.) Christ, being a member of the Godhead, had access to such power.

When Judas and the mob came to the Garden of Gethsemane to capture Christ, He asked them whom they sought. They replied, "Jesus of Nazareth." Jesus replied, as John gives it in the Greek, "*ego eimi*" (John 18:5). Many translators supply the pronoun he, but it is not in the original Greek. Again Christ employed a phrase in such a manner that the Jewish mind could interpret it only one way.

The Greek New Testament also records Christ's use of *ego eimi* in Mark 14:62, Luke 22:70, Matthew 14:27, Mark 6:50, Mark 13:6, and Luke

21:8. In Mark 14:61 the high priest asks Christ if He is " 'the Christ, the Son of the Blessed.' " Jesus replies, " 'I am [*ego eimi*]; and you will see the Son of man sitting at the right hand of Power, and coming with the clouds of heaven' " (verse 62). The high priest immediately accuses Him of blasphemy (verse 64). (See also a parallel account in Luke 22:70.) In Mark 13:6 and Luke 21:8 Christ teaches a similar thought to that of John 13:19, and in Matthew 14:27 and Mark 6:50 He calms the apostles during a storm on the Sea of Galilee. Interestingly, when He reaches the boat, the apostles worship Him and declare, " 'Truly you are the Son of God' " (Matthew 14:33).

Some anti-Trinitarians have argued that Christ occupies a position less than that of the Father. He may be god, but not Almighty God. As the first-created being, He is responsible, they say, for bringing into existence all other creation. But does such a concept fit in with what He and Scripture say about Himself?

If Christ were only the first being the Father formed and did not always exist, He would not have told the Pharisees, " 'Truly, truly, I say to you, before Abraham was, I am.' " Instead He should have said:

"I was"—*ēmēn*
"I came to be"—*egenomēn*
"I had been born"—*egennēthēn*
"I had been created"—*ektisthēn*
"I existed"—*exēsa*

Such expressions would have been grammatically correct, and they would have made more sense if Christ were not Yahweh and eternally existent. But "I am" (*ego eimi*) was definitely the wrong phrase to use. Some have claimed that we must render *ego eimi* in this particular instance as "I have been." That, besides being linguistically unacceptable, creates the question of why the apostle John would have employed such a misleading expression when he could have used a clear, specific one. To accept such an idea forces John into the position of making a stumbling block for the readers of his Gospel.

Christ is not the first being the Father produced, but the "Beginner" or "Originator" (*hē archē*) of creation (Revelation 3:14). *Archē* also appears in Revelation 21:6 where Alpha and Omega obviously cannot be the first created being, but must mean the originator of creation. Jesus is the *prototokos* ("firstborn") in Colossians 1:15, not *protoktisis* or "first created." Scripture uses the position of firstborn to indicate special honor and preeminence. God, for example, calls David and Ephraim His firstborn (Psalm 89:27; Jeremiah 31:9) when they literally were not. Also firstborn may indicate that the Father and the Son have like natures. Something created is quite different from the person who created it, but something born is generally the same as its progenitor. Christ has the same nature as the Father.

The King James Version of the Bible has the apostle John referring to Christ as the "only begotten Son" of God (for example, John 1:14; 3:16; 1

John 4:9). The Revised Standard Version and many other translations render the Greek word *monogenēs* as "only." *Monogenēs* means "the only member of a kin, or kind"; hence generally "only," "single" (Henry George Liddell and Robert Scott, *A Greek-English Lexicon,* Vol. 2, p. 1144). Additional meanings include "unique," "precious," "beloved."

Hebrews 11:17 says that Abraham "was ready to offer up his only [*monogenēs*] son." Yet Isaac was not the patriarch's only son. He had Ishmael plus at least six other children (Genesis 25:1-3). But Isaac was the unique child God promised, the precious, beloved son.

There is no other being in the whole universe like Jesus, the Son of God, who incarnated Himself as a man to save the human race. He is beloved and precious to the Father. And He is eternal, "the same yesterday and today and for ever" (Hebrews 13:8). Christ cannot be a created god because God, the Great I Am, clearly states, "Before me no god was formed, nor shall there be any after me" (Isaiah 43:10).

5

The Humility of God

Some, when confronted with the Bible teaching of Christ's deity, may ask, What about Christ's statements such as "the Father is greater than I" (John 14:28), or what about the fact that He said some things He did not know, but only the Father knew? (See Mark 13:32.) And Christ spoke of His Father as "my God" and "the only true God" (John 20:17; 17:3).

The key to such seeming contradictions comes when we grasp Christ's role on earth and in the plan of salvation. In Philippians 2 Paul outlines how the Christian should behave, citing Christ Himself as the example.

"Have this mind among yourselves," the apostle writes, "which you have in Christ Jesus, who, though he was in the form of God ["who had always been God by nature," Phillips; "had the very nature of God," TEV], did not count equality with God a thing to be grasped ["did not cling to his prerogatives as God's equal," Phillips], but emptied himself, taking the form of a servant, being born in the likeness of men. And being found in human form he humbled himself and became obedient unto death, even death on a cross'' (verses 5-8).

The mere fact that Christ, the Son of God, was incarnated as a human being did not automatically provide salvation for the human race. He had an active role to fulfill. Besides dying on the cross in man's place, He had to live a perfect life—the life Adam and Eve failed to fulfill—and an example the Holy Spirit would help His followers copy. But for human beings to follow that pattern, He could not use any power or ability that mankind did not also have access to.

Called the *kenosis* from the Greek word meaning an act of emptying, the concept declares that Christ denied Himself the use of His divine attributes and powers when He lived a human life. He even performed His miracles through the power supplied Him by the Father (John 5:36). He went so far as to block out His former consciousness and had to develop and learn like all human children. (See Luke 2:40, 52.) But still He was always Yahweh.

As one studies Christ's comments about Himself, especially those which appear to imply that He was less than the Father, one must always judge them in the light of the *kenosis*. It is one of the wonders of Jesus' incarnation that He denied Himself so much.

Yet that is one of the Godhead's characteristics. Some portray God as primarily interested in His own position and power, but God is not like that. He glories in demonstrating His love for others, such as Christ did through the *kenosis*. God considers it His greatest glory.

How do we know? Because someone asked Him what His greatest glory was. God told Moses on Mount Sinai that he had found favor in His sight. In response the Israelite leader dared to request, " 'I pray thee, show me thy glory' " (Exodus 33:18).

The Lord answered Moses' petition by replying, " 'I will make all my goodness pass before you, and will proclaim before you my name "The Lord"; and I will be gracious to whom I will be gracious, and will show mercy on whom I will show mercy' " (Exodus 33:19). Of all the things that God could have offered as His glory, He chose something that involved others. He regarded goodness, graciousness, and mercy as His glory. His glory was His relationship of service to others.

Thus as He passed before Moses, God said, " 'The Lord, the Lord, a God merciful and gracious, slow to anger, and abounding in steadfast love and faithfulness, keeping steadfast love for thousands, forgiving iniquity and transgression and sin' " (Exodus 34:6, 7).

What God presented as His glory, His most majestic trait, was not the power or the abilities at His command. It was not something that directed attention primarily to Himself. He considered His glory not as what others did for Him, nor what He could accomplish that no one else in the universe was capable of, but what He could do *for others*.

This is the greatest trait of the Godhead's character. God constantly seeks to serve others. Never self-centered, He is always other-centered. Unlike the mythical pagan gods who thought only of man's catering to their wishes and who only occasionally bothered to take notice of man's existence, the true God is concerned about His creation. He wants others to love, to care for, which is the reason He created intelligent, living beings in the first place.

God's interest in His creation is more than just that of a Mighty Being overseeing the operation of a vast, complex universe from a distance. He personally involves Himself in the affairs of His created beings. What He is willing to do to serve them brings out His most glorious trait. The Godhead of majesty is also a Godhead of humility. It seems impossible that we could speak of God as being humble, but that is what the Bible reveals.

How can God show humility?

The first Christian martyr, Stephen, gives an insight into one of the ways the Godhead can exhibit humility. Shortly before his death, he—under the inspiration of the Holy Spirit (Acts 7:55)—briefly reviewed the history of Israel. In his speech he described how an angel appeared to Moses in a flaming bush (Acts 7:30). Comparison of Stephen's account of Moses and the burning bush with the Exodus 3 narrative reveals the angel that Stephen mentioned must have been the Lord Himself. (Matching Acts 7:33 with Exodus 3:4, 5 brings out the fact that *God* and *Lord* or *Jehovah* refer to the same being, not two persons as it might seem at first. The Neophyti Targum on Exodus 3 uses ''the Angel of the Lord,'' ''the Word of the Lord,'' and ''the Glory of the Shekinah of the Lord'' as synonymous, interchangeable terms.) God was willing to appear as a lesser being—an angel—in order to communicate with man.

We find a similar case in Genesis 48:16. Shortly before his death, the patriarch Jacob blessed his sons and grandsons, saying, "The angel who has redeemed me from all evil, bless the lads." An angel cannot redeem man from evil. Only God can be a Redeemer and Saviour. The all-powerful God of the whole universe was willing to take the form of an angel—a created being—if by so doing He could help and serve others. He did not consider it beneath His dignity to do so. Many times in the Old Testament the phrase "Angel of the Lord" indicates God's personal intervention in human affairs.

God's humility—His willingness to lower Himself so as to serve others—extended beyond taking the form of an angel, as great a step downward as that might be. Genesis 18 recounts that the Lord came to Abraham in the physical appearance of a man, a creature even lower than an angel. We may resent it when others mistake us for members of a social class supposedly lower than the one we actually belong to, but God was perfectly willing to be seen as a being far below that of the Majestic One. And God willingly humbled Himself even more.

Voluntarily Christ became a man, a member of the most-degraded race in the universe. And when men looked at Him during His life on earth, they did not see some magnificent being such as Adam, the first human, but a person like themselves. The second member of the Godhead, the Son of God, felt pain and thirst and hunger, and He did physical labor to survive like other men and women. Why? To serve others.

Serving others is one of the fundamental principles of the universe. Today we hear much about the ecology crisis—how man is upsetting the balance of life around him. All life exists for the benefit of others. In a pond, for example, the plants absorb sunlight and carbon dioxide and produce food and life-sustaining oxygen. Fish and other animals in the water use the oxygen and eat the food. They give off carbon dioxide, which the plants need. Although a simple illustration, it shows how living things serve each other.

Unfortunately, man has ignored or overlooked the links between living organisms. He has torn the strands that bind all life together. He tries to make nature serve only himself, forgetting that he has a responsibility to take care of it. Thus he ravages natural resources, selfishly dumps his wastes into the air and the water, and unthinkingly destroys any life form that gets in his way.

Unlike mankind, God remembers His obligations to others. In fact, He does not stop with just what a sense of responsibility might dictate. He not only seeks but creates opportunities to show His concern for others.

When man rebelled against God, the Creator could have said that His responsibility to the human race had come to a justifiable end. But God did not stop there. He wanted to do everything possible to bring man back to the relationship he had forfeited. God would not let even His position as supreme ruler of the universe limit His desire to save fallen man. The Son of God humbled Himself to the lowest level, becoming a human being. God's humility embodies His love, His willingness to sacrifice even Himself.

Christ's life was the ultimate example of perfect humility. He came in the spirit of absolute service to mankind and claimed none of the credit for Himself. All possible glory He credited to His Father (John 8:49). "I do not receive glory from men" (John 5:41), He said, and "I do not seek my own glory" (John 8:50). He glorified His Father by His life of service to others (John 17:4). When Christ said, in Matthew 11:29, "I am gentle and lowly in heart," He really meant it.

Humility in service to others forms an ongoing theme in Christ's teaching. He told His disciples that they must "let the greatest among you become as the youngest, and the leader as one who serves." They must follow His example and be "as one who serves" (Luke 22:26, 27). We must always view what the New Testament has to say about Christ in light of His emptying Himself to serve the human race and to set an example for mankind to follow in ministering to each other and to God.

6
God the Holy Spirit

God the Father guided Christ's human life and gave Him the power to perform miracles through the agency of the third member of the Godhead, the Holy Spirit. The divine guidance began to shape Christ's future development when the Holy Spirit overshadowed His mother, Mary, long before His birth (Luke 1:35). The influence on Mary would, of course, extend throughout His childhood. And the Holy Spirit filled Christ Himself, even more so after His baptism by His cousin John the Baptist.

But many through the centuries have regarded the Holy Spirit as only a divine "active force," the power the Father uses to work out His will, but not a conscious, separate personality. Yet if the Spirit is only mindless divine energy, the Bible describes it in a most unusual manner.

First, consider the gender the authors of the New Testament use to refer to the Spirit. Greek, like English, has masculine, feminine, and neuter forms of words (for example, *he, she, it*). But John in such passages as John 14:26 and 16:8, 13-15 employs the masculine form of the pronoun referring to the Spirit—*ekeinos* instead of the neuter *ekeino*. If the

Holy Spirit were only a "force" or "influence," the apostle should have used the neuter gender. John is misleading his readers unless he clearly meant what his choice of gender implies.

Second, Scripture constantly mentions characteristics which fit only a conscious being. To cite a few examples, the Bible says that the Spirit—

1. Speaks (Revelation 2:7; Acts 13:2).
2. Makes intercession (Romans 8:26).
3. Calls, oversees, commands (Acts 16:6, 7; 20:28).
4. May be grieved (Ephesians 4:30).
5. May be insulted, "outraged" (Hebrews 10:29).
6. Can be lied to (Acts 5:3).
7. Can be blasphemed and sinned against (Matthew 12:31, 32).
8. Teaches (John 14:26).
9. Glorifies Christ (John 16:14).
10. Counsels (John 14:16).

Romans 8:27 talks about "the mind of the Spirit." Do forces or influences have minds? Some may suggest that the Bible writers merely used personification, but the pattern is too consistent and too strong to support that idea. They would have hardly equated a personified force with two actual beings as Matthew did in the baptismal formula (Matthew 28:19), or as Paul did in the apostolic benediction (2 Corinthians 13:14).

Paul in Acts 28:25 declared, " 'The Holy Spirit was right in saying to your fathers through Isaiah the prophet . . . ' " (Isaiah 6:9, 10 quoted, a passage which begins, ''And I heard the voice of the Lord saying, 'Whom shall I send, and who will go for us?' '' [Isaiah 6:8]).

Jewish Targums used the Holy Spirit as a substitute for *Yahweh* when referring to God's speaking to Israel. And Scripture indicates that the Spirit is also God as much as is the Father or the Son, having such traits as omniscience (1 Corinthians 2:10) and the ability to be omnipresent (Psalm 139:7). As His special responsibility, He guides the mind of the Christian and brings it into harmony with the divine will, or as the Bible would phrase it, ''fills'' him. (See typical passages as Acts 2:4, 33.) In fact, Paul classifies all human beings into two categories: those who have the Holy Spirit dwelling in them and those who don't. He refers to ''those who live according to the flesh'' and ''those who live according to the Spirit'' (Romans 8:5). One group he calls ''in the flesh'' and says that they ''cannot please God'' (Romans 8:8). They face eternal destruction (Romans 8:6). But the other group —labeled ''in the Spirit''—will receive eternal life and happiness.

The presence of the Holy Spirit is the absolutely necessary criterion for being a follower of God. Paul declares, ''You are in the Spirit, if the Spirit of God really dwells in you. Any one who does not have the Spirit of Christ does not belong to him'' (Romans 8:9). Paul is not talking about the nature or characteristics of Christ but the Third Member of the Godhead as Romans 8 makes undeniably clear. With the Holy Spirit every Christian becomes a son of God through divine adoption (Romans 8:14; Galatians 4:5, 6). Any Christian group that sees no need for the Holy Spirit or believes that God has limited it to a few select ones, condemns its followers to eternal death. Their belief comes close to that warned against in Matthew 12:31, 32. What the Holy Spirit does in us is the key to our sanctification and salvation.

7

The Significance of the Trinity

Within the limited space of this small book we can consider only part of the Biblical evidence for the Trinity. But it should be enough for the reader to see clearly that the Trinity is a Biblical doctrine. But what significance does it have for the individual Christian? Is it just an intellectual curiosity for theologians to ponder? Actually the doctrine of the Trinity helps us understand a number of things about God and the plan of salvation.

Critics of Christianity have occasionally charged that the Biblical story of salvation portrays a great injustice. They claim that it states that one being (God) took the punishment of a guilty being (Adam) and placed it on a third, innocent being (Christ). But the concept of the Godhead does away with this seeming problem. The members of the Godhead did not put divine punishment on another, but They agreed among Themselves to accept it, Christ volunteering as Their representative.

The doctrine of the Trinity answers the question where the ability to love and communicate comes from. Some have suggested that before God created other beings, love existed only as an abstract ideal or concept in God's mind. But that is a pagan concept borrowed from the Greeks. Abstractions have no existence. Yet love did exist before God made other beings, because the members of the Godhead could and did love one another. Jesus stated that the Father had loved Him before the foundation of the world (John 17:24). They loved in active, concrete ways.

Those who do not believe in a personal God have a hard time explaining where the ability to communicate evolved from in an impersonal universe. God, however, is personal—in fact, God is Three Persons. And persons can communicate with each other.

Also the Trinity answers the philosophical problem of how we can find both unity and diversity in the universe. God created man in His image. There is a unity of mankind. Each individual belongs to and makes up a whole; yet each human being is also an entity uniquely his own. That is the way it is with the Trinity.

We talk about the Father's great sacrifice and love in sending His Son to die in rebellious man's place. But if Christ were less than God, the Father's love was anything but infinite. John 3:16 would not really mean that much because God's love would not be absolute. If Christ were not a full member of the Godhead, equal in all ways with the Father before the Incarnation, then man can conceive of a greater sacrifice than God actually made. The Trinitarian sees one of the Godhead Himself accepting humanity's punishment. Here is total love. Can man have higher and loftier thoughts than God? If Christ

were not equal to God and an intimate part of the
Godhead, He was—to use an analogy—the Father's
first and favorite piece of art. Christ would be of
great sentimental value but replaceable. God could
have created another Christ just as a man with a
ruined sculpture can carve another.

And if Christ were not fully God, the Father
stands accused by Satan that His love was not suffi-
cient to make a supreme sacrifice. The love of God is
infinitely greater when Yahweh the Son dies than
when the Father assigns the mission to a lesser
being. God rules by love, and because His love is
suspect, so is His authority. But the doctrine of the
Trinity teaches us that the Godhead did make the
ultimate sacrifice. Christ had "the whole fulness of
deity" dwelling in Him (Colossians 2:9).

Christ declared that "no one knows the Father
except the Son and any one to whom the Son chooses
to reveal him" (Matthew 11:27). Only God can
comprehend and know how to communicate about
Him. Christ was God. Now God the Holy Spirit is
revealing and communicating God to us.

Many have rejected the Godhead, the Trinity,
because it involves concepts we cannot completely
explain. Only God can explain God, and we would
need the mind of God to understand. Man has con-
tinually failed to grasp the fact that what we *can*
comprehend is *not* the whole of reality. We understand only a small fraction of the universe, but few
would be so foolish as to deny that the rest of it exists
because we cannot explain everything about it.

Human reason is extremely limited. Men once

scoffed at the idea that the earth races through space. Why? Because they could not understand how this could be. It was not reasonable, and they could give some seemingly strong objections against it. If the earth moved, to cite some of their arguments, the wind which its movement created would blow everything off the planet's surface. Dropped objects would not fall straight down as we see them do, but at a curving slant as we know today a bomb does when released from a speeding airplane. To medieval men a moving earth appeared to contradict all reason. Yet we now know they were wrong. Reality was larger and greater than what their minds could conceive.

Perhaps we can compare the Godhead to a divine committee of equals but with specific areas of responsibility. It is also a synergy, a situation where the whole is greater than the sum of its parts, as a man is much more than a collection of chemicals, cells, tissues, and organs. The Godhead has unity so close that we can rightly refer to its members as one God. But whatever analogy we employ, it but barely scratches the surface in explaining what the Godhead is, and can also be misleading in certain details. We may argue that the Godhead does not exist because we cannot dissect and explain it like some specimen under a microscope. Yet to do so is to become like the ancient pagan who could conceive of his god only as like himself. The Christian has an infinite God.